DK READERS

Level 3

Shark Attack!
Beastly Tales
Titanic
Invaders from Outer Space
Movie Magic
Time Traveler
Bermuda Triangle
Tiger Tales
Plants Bite Back!
Zeppelin: The Age of the Airship
Spies
Terror on the Amazon
Disasters at Sea
The Story of Anne Frank
Abraham Lincoln: Lawyer, Leader, Legend
George Washington: Soldier, Hero, President
Extreme Sports
Spiders' Secrets
The Big Dinosaur Dig
Space Heroes: Amazing Astronauts
The Story of Chocolate
School Days Around the World
Polar Bear Alert!
Welcome to China

My First Ballet Show
Ape Adventures
Greek Myths
Amazing Animal Journeys
Spacebusters: The Race to the Moon
WWE: Triple H
WWE: Undertaker
Star Wars: Star Pilot
Star Wars: I Want to Be a Jedi
Star Wars: The Story of Darth Vader
Star Wars: Yoda in Action
Star Wars: Forces of Darkness
Marvel Heroes: Amazing Powers
The X-Men School
Pokémon: Explore with Ash and Dawn
Pokémon: Become a Pokémon Trainer
The Invincible Iron Man: Friends and Enemies
Wolverine: Awesome Powers
Abraham Lincoln: Abogado, Líder, Leyenda
    en español
Al Espacio: La Carrera a la Luna
    en español
Fantastic Four: The World's Greatest Superteam
Fantastic Four: Adversaries

Level 4

Earthquakes and Other Natural Disasters
Days of the Knights
Secrets of the Mummies
Pirates! Raiders of the High Seas
Horse Heroes
Micro Monsters
Going for Gold!
Extreme Machines
Flying Ace: The Story of Amelia Earhart
Robin Hood
Black Beauty
Free at Last! The Story of Martin Luther King, Jr.
Joan of Arc
Spooky Spinechillers
Welcome to The Globe! The
    Story of Shakespeare's Theater
Space Station: Accident on Mir
Antarctic Adventure
Atlantis: The Lost City?
Dinosaur Detectives
Danger on the Mountain: Scaling the World's
    Highest Peaks
Crime Busters
The Story of Muhammad Ali
First Flight: The Story of the Wright Brothers
D-Day Landings: The Story of the Allied Invasion
Solo Sailing
Thomas Edison: The Great Inventor
Dinosaurs! Battle of the Bones
Skate!
Snow Dogs! Racers of the North
JLA: Batman's Guide to Crime and Detection
JLA: Superman's Guide to the Universe
JLA: Aquaman's Guide to the Oceans
JLA: Wonder Woman's Book of Myths
JLA: Flash's Book of Speed

JLA: Green Lantern's Book of Inventions
The Story of the X-Men: How it all Began
Creating the X-Men: How Comic Books
    Come to Life
Spider-Man's Amazing Powers
The Story of Spider-Man
The Incredible Hulk's Book of Strength
The Story of the Incredible Hulk
Transformers: The Awakening
Transformers: The Quest
Transformers: The Unicron Battles
Transformers: The Uprising
Transformers: Megatron Returns
Transformers: Terrorcon Attack
Star Wars: Galactic Crisis!
Star Wars: Beware the Dark Side
Star Wars: Epic Battles
Star Wars: Jedi Adventures
Marvel Heroes: Greatest Battles
Rise of the Iron Man
The Story of Wolverine
Fantastic Four: Evil Adversaries
Graphic Readers: The Price of Victory
Graphic Readers: The Terror Trail
Graphic Readers: Curse of the Crocodile God
Graphic Readers: Instruments of Death
Graphic Readers: The Spy-Catcher Gang
Graphic Readers: Wagon Train Adventure
Los Asombrosos Poderes de Spider-Man en español
La Historia de Spider-Man en español

A Note to Parents

DK READERS is a compelling program for beginning readers, designed in conjunction with leading literacy experts, including Dr. Linda Gambrell, Distinguished Professor of Education at Clemson University. Dr. Gambrell has served as President of the National Reading Conference, the College Reading Association, and the International Reading Association.

Beautiful illustrations and superb full-color photographs combine with engaging, easy-to-read stories to offer a fresh approach to each subject in the series. Each DK READER is guaranteed to capture a child's interest while developing his or her reading skills, general knowledge, and love of reading.

The five levels of DK READERS are aimed at different reading abilities, enabling you to choose the books that are exactly right for your child:

Pre-level 1: Learning to read
Level 1: Beginning to read
Level 2: Beginning to read alone
Level 3: Reading alone
Level 4: Proficient readers

The "normal" age at which a child begins to read can be anywhere from three to eight years old. Adult participation through the lower levels is very helpful for providing encouragement, discussing storylines, and sounding out unfamiliar words.

No matter which level you select, you can be sure that you are helping your child learn to read, then read to learn!

LONDON, NEW YORK, MUNICH,
MELBOURNE, AND DELHI

Project Editor Caroline Greene
Art Editor Rebecca Johns
Senior Art Editor Cheryl Telfer
Series Editor Deborah Lock
US Editor Regina Kahney
Production Editor Sean Daly
Picture Researcher Jo Haddon
Jacket Designer Natalie Godwin
Publishing Manager Bridget Giles
Indexer Lynn Bresler
Natural History Consultant
Paul Hillyard

Reading Consultant
Linda B. Gambrell, Ph.D.

First American Edition, 2002
This edition, 2010
10 11 12 13 14 15 10 9 8 7 6 5 4 3 2 1
Published in the United States by DK Publishing
375 Hudson Street, New York, New York 10014

DK books are available at special discounts when purchased
in bulk for sales promotions, premiums,
fund-raising, or educational use.
For details, contact: DK Publishing Special Markets
375 Hudson Street, New York, New York 10014
SpecialSales@dk.com

A catalog record for this book is available
from the Library of Congress
ISBN: 978-0-7566-6283-7 (Paperback)
ISBN: 978-0-7566-6284-4 (Hardcover)

Color reproduction by Colourscan, Singapore
Printed and bound in China by L Rex Printing Co., Ltd.

The publisher would like to thank the following for
their kind permission to reproduce their images:
Position key: c=center, t=top, b=bottom, l=left, r=right.
Bruce Coleman Ltd: Andrew Purcell 27tc. **Corbis:** Alastair Shay, Papilio
6bl; Anthony Bannister 12tl; Archivo Iconografico, SA 13tr; Buddy Mays
21; Joe McDonald 42-43; Reuters NewMedia Inc. 18tc. **FLPA - Images of
nature:** M Moffett/Minden Pictures 19c; Silvestri Fotoservice 33. **Alfonso
Lazo:** 13bc, 13bc. **N.H.P.A:** Daniel Heuclin 5cra, 21tr, 24-25; James
Carmichael 14-15, 15tltr; Laurie Campbell 36-37; Stephen Dalton 26tl,
32br, 35tr, 40bc; Steve Robinson 10-11. **Oxford Scientific Films:** Bob
Parks 10bc; Colin Milkins 43tr; David Boag 34br; G I Bernard 44bc;
Harry Fox 28bc; J A L Cooke 17bc, 26bl; 31; John Mitchell 25crb; London
Scientific Films 38-39. **Science Photo Library:** Claude Nuridsany & Marie
Perennou 5cla, 29c; Martin Dohrn 40cl, 41; Pascal Goetheluck 9; Simon
D Pollard 45, 46-47. **Woodfall Wild Images:** Bob Gibbons 7.
Jacket images: Front: **naturepl.com:** Niall Benvie cb (spider);
Rolf Nussbaumer (web background)
All other images © Dorling Kindersley Limited
For further information see: www.dkimages.com

Discover more at
www.dk.com

Contents

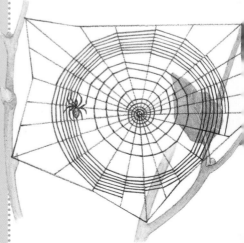

DK READERS

READING
3
ALONE

Spiders'
Secrets

Written by Richard Platt

DK Publishing

World-wide web

Spiders are everywhere. There are more than 30,000 different kinds living around the world. Find out about the amazing secret lives of six different spiders. Watch how one tiny spider spins its sticky web, which can catch a much bigger insect for supper. Discover how spiders adapt to living in all sorts of conditions— even underwater.

NORTH AMERICA

ATLANTIC OCEAN

PACIFIC OCEAN

SOUTH AMERICA

Tarantula: I thrive in tropical rainforests. Meet me on page 12.

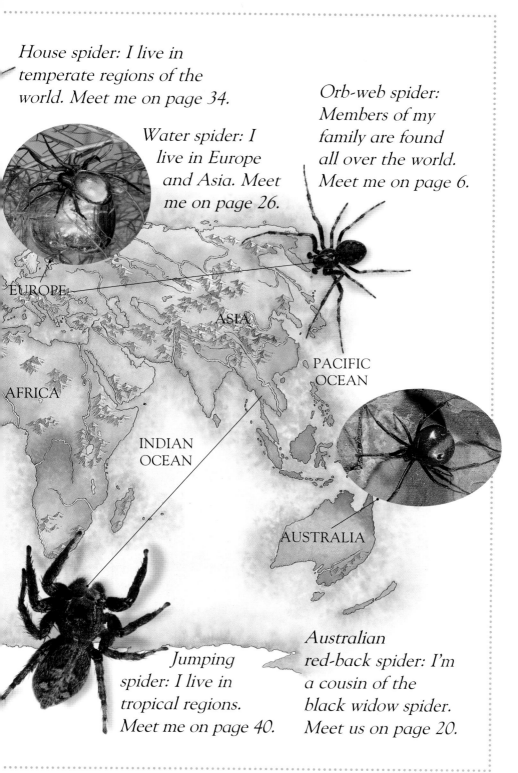

House spider: I live in temperate regions of the world. Meet me on page 34.

Water spider: I live in Europe and Asia. Meet me on page 26.

Orb-web spider: Members of my family are found all over the world. Meet me on page 6.

EUROPE

ASIA

AFRICA

PACIFIC OCEAN

INDIAN OCEAN

AUSTRALIA

Jumping spider: I live in tropical regions. Meet me on page 40.

Australian red-back spider: I'm a cousin of the black widow spider. Meet us on page 20.

5

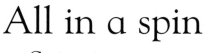

All in a spin

Spinning a new web is hard work for me, but it's fun to watch for you. You'll see me at my busiest early on a misty fall morning in a field or park. I am an orb-web spider and my web is a clever trap. "Orb" means a ring or circle, which describes my web's shape. The fine silk threads are coated with sticky goo to snare my insect food. Dewdrops on my web help you to see the threads.

Orb-web spider

There are many different orb-web spiders. This one signs its web with a zig-zag.

Some orb-web spiders have dotted patterns on their backs.

1. To make my web
I fix the first thread
between two twigs.
I tighten the thread
and spin a looser one
below. From its middle,
I lower myself down.

2. I fix the thread that
lowered me to a twig
below. Then I run up and
down, adding to the web
to make a kind of frame.

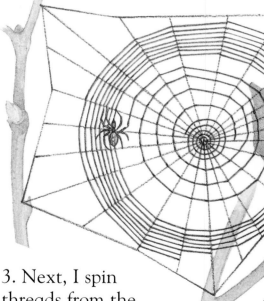

3. Next, I spin
threads from the
center, out to the
edges. These look like
the spokes of a wheel.

4. I climb from
spoke to spoke,
laying a spiral that
adds strength. Then
I lay another spiral
coated with gluey drops
to make the web sticky.

If webs lasted forever, it would be an easy life, but lots of things spoil them. Rain, wind, and animals break webs. Dust takes the stickiness away. So each day, I have to start building and repairing my web again! Luckily, not all of my effort is wasted. I can eat up the threads and recycle them into fresh silk, which I spin from the spinnerets on my back.

But please don't touch our webs unless you are a fly. Then you are VERY welcome!

Super-strong silk
Spider silk is twice as strong as steel of the same thickness. Yet the silk is very light. A thread around the world would weigh just 12 ounces (340 grams).

spinnerets

Once my trap is set, I rest and wait. I cannot see much because I have bad eyesight, but I have a very good sense of touch. I can feel when my net catches an insect.

Senses

Most spiders have bad eyesight, but they sense vibrations when something lands in their webs.

I scuttle into action and reach my victim in a few seconds. To stop my meal from wriggling, I wrap it up in silk. Then I kill it with a single bite. Dinner is served! I crush the insect's body with my jaws and squirt in digestive juice. Before long everything inside has turned to insect soup, which I can drink. Delicious!

Orb-web spider with dragonfly prey

Hairy and scary

We tarantulas come from a big family. Mostly you'll find us in North and South America, but we have cousins in Africa and Australia, too. We're the world's biggest spiders—my legs could stretch right across a dinner plate.

Baboon spider—an African tarantula

Tarantulas are very hairy spiders.

Dancing cure

People in Italy used to think that you could cure a tarantula bite by performing a wild dance called the tarantella.

There is a kind of hairy spider that lives near Taranto in Italy. Nowadays it is known as the wolf spider, but it used to be called a tarantula, after the town. When Italians first went to live in the Americas, they called the hairy spiders there tarantulas. So that's how we got our name.

Wolf spider from southern Italy

Like other spiders, I spin silk, but I don't need a web to catch food. All I have to do is wait for lunch to walk past my burrow and then I pounce. I catch mostly crickets, beetles, and other insects.

A Peruvian tarantula eating a lizard.

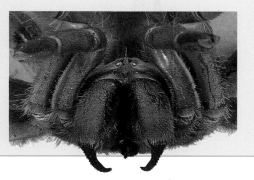

Sometimes I eat bigger animals, such as mice or snakes. My Australian cousins live on small birds and bats. We can kill these creatures because we have special fangs that stab. But I wouldn't attack you unless you frightened me. My bite doesn't kill you, but it does make you very sore.

Tarantula

Yes! I'm big and
hairy. So what? Spiders cannot
shave. Besides, the hairs keep us
warm and protect us. They sense
vibrations when enemies are close.

This hairy skin was new yesterday. I have to change it often, because I quickly grow out of it. When I feel cramped in my skin, I pump myself up so that it cracks. I pull myself out and there's a new skin underneath. It is called molting and it's like pulling fingers out of a glove. I can't defend myself while I do it, so I seal up my burrow with silk to keep out enemies.

A tarantula pulling itself out of its old skin.

Perhaps you think we are horrible?
Not everyone agrees. In fact, some
people keep us as pets. Just think of
us as gerbils with four extra legs!
In some ways, we make better pets
than gerbils. We are clean, we don't
smell, and female tarantulas live much
longer than most other pets. I am only
ten years old now and I could live for
another 20 years.

If you want to keep a tame tarantula, choose carefully. Some of us are very rare. Make sure the spider you buy was raised in captivity and not caught in the wild.

Some tarantulas walk on water. Air trapped by their hairs helps them to float.

Watch out, Dad!

Let me introduce myself. People call me the black widow spider. Would you like me to explain my strange name? All in good time. I have other things to tell you.

I live in Arizona where the gardens swarm with delicious insects and any outside bathrooms are full of tasty flies. Spiders just like me live in southern Europe and Australia, too.

We have shiny black bodies with red markings. You will have to look hard to see them, though, because I am tiny. I would easily fit on the smallest coin. Despite my small size, I am very famous. I am one of the most poisonous spiders in the world.

Deadlier than the male

Female black widows are much bigger than their mates. The bite of the male spider is never deadly to people.

This black widow spider has a red egg-timer pattern underneath its belly.

My poison is 15 times stronger than a rattlesnake's. It harms large animals, but don't worry! I rarely kill humans. We bite when we are in danger of getting squashed.

A black widow spider climbing into a plant pot.

Fight the bite
A doctor can give an injection of drugs, called antivenins, to fight the black widow spider's poison.

Poisonous spider bites are rare. My bite may not be felt at first, but soon

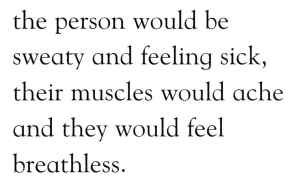

the person would be sweaty and feeling sick, their muscles would ache and they would feel breathless.

I am shy and I live in dark places, like empty boxes, cans, or pots. Shoes make nice nests. So shake that shoe. And watch where you are sitting!

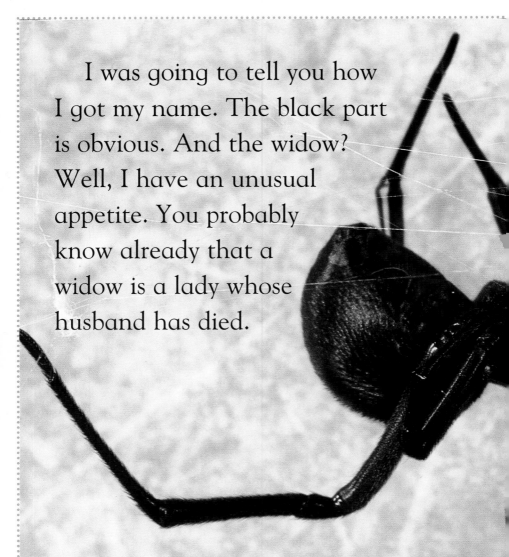

I was going to tell you how
I got my name. The black part
is obvious. And the widow?
Well, I have an unusual
appetite. You probably
know already that a
widow is a lady whose
husband has died.

To lay eggs and produce more
spiders, I need to find a male to mate
with. Mating makes me hungry, and
a male black widow is a tasty snack.
So, I sometimes eat my partner.

It seems cruel, but I'm only thinking of the children. At least their dad gives them a good start in life by feeding their mother!

Black widow spider with eggs and young

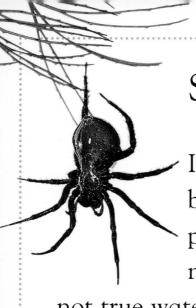

Super scuba

I am a male water spider. I spend almost all my time beneath the surface of a pond. Other spiders live near water, but they are not true water spiders. Many can walk on water. Some can dive. One spider splashes with its legs to attract fish. But I live under the water. Breathing isn't a problem because I carry an air supply, like a human scuba diver.

A water spider traps air in a bubble so that it can breathe.

Air bubbles turn the spider's body silver.

I swim to the surface and push my bottom out. Air sticks to the hairs on my body and becomes a bubble. I take this bubble with me and breathe the trapped air when I dive down again.

I build my web under the water, too, on water plants. I don't use the web to trap food. Instead I use it as a nest, and fill it with air. To do this, I swim to the surface and catch a large bubble between my back legs. It is bigger than the bubble I use for breathing. Then I carry it to my nest, using threads of silk to pull myself down. The web turns silver as it fills with air. Oxygen gas from the plants keeps the air fresh.

A male water spider inside his air bubble.

Scientists call this spider Argyroneta (AR-gee-ro-NET-a) a name made from Latin words that mean "with a silvery net."

I live underwater because of all the food there. I eat shrimps and the young of insects. I also enjoy tiny fish. I'm a hunter, you see. If a tasty snack comes within reach I dart out and capture it. I kill it with a bite from my poisonous fangs. Then I carry my catch back to my nest. To feed, I turn my victim's body to liquid using my digestive juice.

Why do I go home for meals, instead of having an underwater picnic? Because you can't eat soup underwater! The water would wash the liquid away. I don't lose a drop in my nest.

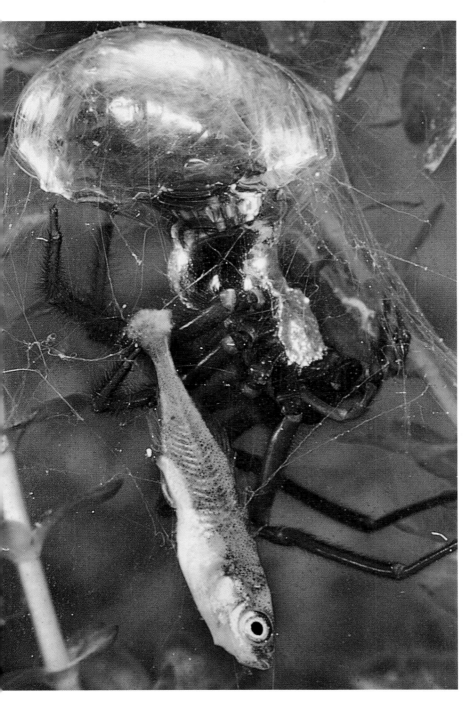

A water spider catching a fish.

31

In spring, I look for a female spider to start a family. When I find her, I build a new nest next door. I spin a web tunnel, linking the two nests. Then I scurry through to mate. The female does not lay her eggs immediately. First, she builds an air-filled nursery on top of her own nest. Next, she lays her eggs inside a special white bag. Then she seals the entrance with silk. Her spiderlings hatch out nearly a month later. They breathe air trapped in the nursery until they grow big enough to make nests of their own.

Tiny swimmers
Male water spiders are a little bigger than females: a pair would fit easily on a postage stamp.

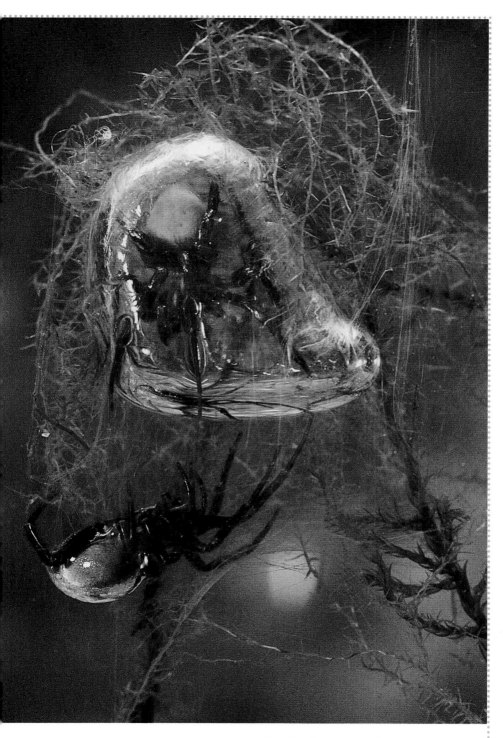

Spiderlings in the nursery

House guests

House spider

I remember you! You tried to step on me, but you weren't quick enough. House spiders like me are the fastest sprinters on eight legs. We are great travelers, too. When people first sailed from Europe to America, we went with them. Now we have family all over the United States and Europe.

Wet but not drowned
House spiders can survive a soaking in cold water. Though it might look like they've drowned, they will be fine once they dry out.

If you find a spider
in your bathroom, it will not be
a female like me. We stay close to the
web. No, it will be a foolish male house
spider. Some spiders have hairy feet that
grip shiny slopes, but a house spider does
not. He loses his grip on the surface of
a bathtub, slides in, and cannot escape.
Don't scream and run from the room
when you find him. He won't harm you.
Just drape a towel over the edge and he
will climb out.

    In case you forget that I share
your house, I leave cobwebs as little
reminders. You may think my webs are
dirty, useless things, but to me, each one
is home sweet home. All right, I admit
my web is a mess, but it catches flies just
as well as the prettiest orb spider's web.

A male house spider catching a fly.

Do you know how something so fine as my cobweb can last for years? It's because I coat each thread with chemicals to keep the silk from rotting. The chemicals are antibiotics, like the drugs your doctor sometimes gives you when you are sick.

Of course nobody wants cobwebs everywhere. They gather dust and make a house look dirty. But think before you get out the vacuum cleaner. Do you really have to clear away ALL my webs? If you leave a few, I will work hard for you. I will guard your house against other spiders that can give you nasty bites. (I keep them out by eating their food and by taking the best places to build webs.) I will catch the flies that spread germs, too.

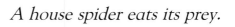

A house spider eats its prey.

My webs also trap furniture beetles, which you call woodworms. I do all this as well as any insect spray and I do it without any harmful chemicals, and free of charge!

Jumping Jack

Keep still! I have spotted a cricket. If you don't scare it, I will soon have a delicious snack. Most spiders wait for their meals to walk by, but not me. I go out hunting high in the trees of the rainforest.

Olympic leaper
Some jumping spiders can leap 40 times their length. If they were human, they'd be able to clear three tennis courts.

I am called a jumping spider because that is how I hunt. When I see something tasty I creep toward it with the stealth of a cat. I wait. Then I spring! Before I leap, I spin out a safety rope of silk, just in case I miss my target. But I don't miss very often.

These are two photographs joined together to show how the spider leaps onto its prey.

To spot my victims, I need sharp eyes, and lots of them! I have eight altogether. The three smaller pairs give me all-around vision. I can spot danger ahead, behind, and on both sides, all at once.

The two headlights
at the front are my
hunting eyes. They
are super-sharp.
They let me see in
three dimensions and
in color, just like your
eyes. You will see
them change color as
I look around. When
they turn black, that
means I am looking
straight at YOU!

My bright markings make me one of the most colorful spiders in the world. Surely even you find me hard to resist? However, not all male jumping spiders are colored like parrots. Many of us are quite drab. And some of us are brilliant mimics. For instance, a few of my cousins look like leaves and twigs. You would never spot them on the rainforest floor.

We also disguise ourselves as beetles and ants. It's a clever way to avoid being eaten by birds. Spiders are tasty, but the ants and beetles we imitate taste horrible, so birds leave us alone.

A jumping spider disguised as an ant.

A multi-colored jumping spider

When it is time to find a mate, I start the same way every spider does. I follow my noses! Yes, NOSES, for I have many of them. I sense smells through lots of tiny holes on my legs. A female spider leaves her scent on a thread of silk, which she spins as she moves.

When I sniff her silk, I know I am on her trail. Once I have tracked her down, I start to dance. I wave my front legs in the air and run sideways. Soon she is under my spell. Darling! Let's make beautiful spiderlings together!

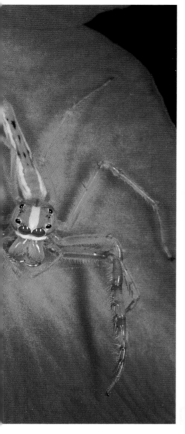

Male (left) and female (right) jumping spiders

Jumping spiders come in many shapes, colors, and sizes.

Glossary

Antibiotic
A healing drug.

Antivenin
A drug that fights
the effects of a
poisonous bite.

Captivity
The condition of an
animal raised and
kept by humans.

Cobweb
Another name for
web—the trap or
home that spiders
make with their silk.

Cricket
A long-legged
jumping insect.

Dewdrop
A drop of water
that collects on
objects outside on
a still, clear night.

Digestive juice
The fluid that
animals produce to
turn solid food into
a liquid, which their
bodies can absorb.

Disguise
When an animal
has the color or
shape of another
animal to fool
other creatures.

Fang
A long, pointed,
sharp tooth.

Gerbil
A furry rodent from
Asia and Africa
often kept as a pet.

Molt
To throw off an
outer skin and
replace it with a
new one that has
grown underneath.

Nursery
A special room
for babies, and
a specially-made
web for raising
baby spiders.

Orb-web
A web that has
a circular shape.

Oxygen
A gas found in air
and water that all
animals need to
stay alive.

Poison
A chemical causing
illness or death.

Prey
An animal hunted
or captured for
food by another
animal.

Scuba
A tank of air and
a face mask that
allows divers to
breathe underwater.
Water spiders create
their own scubas by
using an air bubble.

Silk
A fine thread
produced by insects,
including spiders.

Spiderling
The name for
a baby spider.

Spinnerets
The body parts that
spiders use to make
silk for their webs.

Spoke
A thread linking the
outside of a web to
its center.

Temperate region
Area with a climate
that is neither very
hot nor very cold.

Tropical rainforest
Thick forest in
warm, damp regions
near the equator
(the earth's middle).

Vibration
A shaking or
quivering.

Index